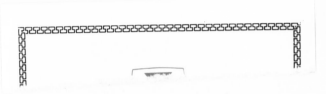

D1074042

AN OBERON BOOK

This is to the memory of Louis Hoffma
and to the memory of eac
of my other grandparen

also for their childre

CHAIM THE SLAUGHTERER

JOSEPH SHERMAN

PROBLEMS OF MY OWN

ask an indian
to define a *Canadian*
he will
tell you what
he was

ask an anglo-canadian
to define a *Canadian*
he will
tell you what
he is

ask a québecois
to define a *Canadian*
he will
tell you what
he should be

ask a jew
to define a *Canadian*
he will

laugh

THE NAMING OF NAMES

I am Jonathan
Or could have been
But for my great-grandfather
Who was dead

Named for the sound of a name
Instead of blood
I might have been
But for my grandmother
Who insisted

I am Jonathan
Or could have been
But for my mother
Who complied

Eight letters in my name
Instead of six
I could have had
But for my father
Who compromised

I am Jonathan
Or could have been
But for me
Who would not cleave in two

FOR MORDECAI RICHLER'S SHALINSKY WHO SAID "A JEW IS AN IDEA"

In the days before
the synagogue's fire   when I was thirteen
I would take such a thought as this
a problem worth a morning's pondering
to the Shul
to the dusty corner next the Ark
where sat Epstein
beneath his grey homburg   *reading*
tucked within the folds of his yellowing Tallith
(a shawl that could canopy a wedding party)
I would go to his seat before opening prayers
and put it all to him   this man
who could love his people no more
if he lived as long again
And I can see old Epstein place his finger
in the book of prayer   close it
and look up
Epstein who was master of a good six tongues
not counting Yiddish and Hebrew
would say   with a confidant's smile
so I could understand
"You know, eh, that the Creator
(whose Name we cannot pronounce)
made the heaven and earth in six days,
and before He rested on the seventh
which He made especially holy, eh, as He should,

you know this? that on the morning of the sixth day
He rubbed the dust between His fingers and said,
and this I tell you now He said, 'You know,
I have got a Wonderful Idea!' "

MR. PEANUT

Once   a long summer ago
when the heavy sun was shining through a bottle
I ran down a Bridgewater street
and afternoon   ran after Mr. Peanut
who had dropped his cane
from the dance he was dancing
on the back of a flat-bed truck

I ran buttered in summer
past all children put together
hugging what I had picked up
getting nearer and nearer   reaching out
with my extended length
with the witch-black cane to the dancer dancing

and as he bent to receive me
I could see through his eyes
that there was nothing   save a shell
an empty pod   with holes
for arms and holes for eyes
and a man inside
a dry paper peanut
with monocle, top hat and tuxedo trousers

Poor Mr. Peanut
what had they done for their money
but gutted you and left only room for a man
a twitching ersatz dancing fool
on the back of a moving flat-bed truck
pulling away from a small boy   without a cane
standing alone on a Bridgewater street
on an end-of-August afternoon

O such a fool what a fool you were
to pretend you knew me

THE AMAZING CANNON AT LIVERPOOL, N.S.

Liverpool has the greatest cannon in the world
>aged   firm   resolute

their backs fitting snugly
>between a small boy's knees
>bare legs rubbing each mottled flank

with terrible ridged mouths
>set to rattle navies

I recall two
>facing against the thin steady waves

and me crouched low along a black spine
>eyes following the angle of the snout
>out over the heads of all others
>walking along distantly
>over the frail pebbles

From my very first lookout till my last
>I searched for sail
>till my eyes gave in

then for a radio mast
>and finally in desperation
>for the bare flick of an oar
>sneaking through the fog

anything on which to unleash my power

but my ship never came in at Liverpool
and I could only imagine
the shock
of action
the hot beach laced with smoke

I learned to accept the cannon for that

Over the years I felt more daring
perched high and vulnerable
then I felt fear
holding that beach

eventually I was simply alone
and not so high

ESTHER I

Of all in my family
        I most admire my grandmother—my mother's mother
and miss her as one does
the exposed warm core of a good near-legend
stored away

As a convent student she painted and was a fine artist
(though she never realized it—never seemed to), until
she married and redirected her artistry;
and I dream she would see it in me
clear as I would see the pride in her

We own curling photos of her, younger even than the day
my grandfather (her cousin) told her he would marry her
—she too young to care, he old enough to know better
and did, for he was right and sure at eighteen—
and in the nine years it took to bear him out
my grandmother learned to be 21 and as right
and sure
        and even more assertive

In her years she became the family rock
to whom all the sensible were somehow tied—she provided
and was shelter,
        giving advice, guidance, even money; giving
birth and love,
        with love more plentiful than the money—
taking every year to plan and give away the thousands
of a never-won Sweepstakes prize; a Jewish lady
who issued Christmas baskets anonymously,
at 57 taking much too long a time watching
the red of her blood turn to water
        —knowing and smiling pain

Because I am not that strong
I especially miss her,
so when I am 57 her memory will have grown
to proportions reserved for those biblical chapters
in which I might believe,
if her own religion had been anything but charity

I wish the grandchildren and great-grandchildren
she could not know
to examine her photograph, and the resources
behind the lips and eyes and hands,
to discover
      held unsprung
her all-too-numerable moments and schemes for moments,
that read and tell as imperfect dreaming,
worn always like that visceral jewelry
her love

     It was
at the time of her death, all
that was not white and horrible

THE ONLY GAME IN TOWN

As we were choosing up sides
the only other Jewish boy
in Bridgewater
winked me aside
and told me what he was

Later
when I shot him
it was with more pleasure
and less guilt
than I would have thought possible

KASHRUT: AN OBSERVATION

I studied the slaughterer
Stroking each bird with the blade
As he breathed (a life drawn with each breath
Or perhaps he breathed only with each stroke)

In that time between
His touch and the blood
It was possible to retain belief
In the life of the chicken

WHAT WE LOOK FOR, WHO WE FIND

Sam Greene
who was always old and bald and toothless
one day became conspicuously one-legged, yet
matter-of-factly continued to run his ice-cream parlour
tobacco and candy store, a den dusty
with corpulent shadows where he dealt in two flavours
of grey ice cream, variously sized and packaged other
materials—sunbleached—once chocolate (cigarettes
cigars cigarillos Sailor's Tobacco as well) and
more important and less prosaically
continued running that poker game of a nearly
perpetual nature, set about one vast circuital table,
situated to the rear of the shadowy den next
the room where he slept, off Victoria Road
—that room perhaps escaping the cast of the green
coned lamp, its hovering incandescence seeping
insipidly over the game's edge and the baize horizon
to vanish in the ocean of surrounding darkness.

  Half in that light
  were such as my father, and other men
  to whom the atmosphere, dimmed and clouded
  as it was by their coiling smoke
  and the continuous hazy fall of sloughed ash,
  lent a mysterious garb of novelty, made one
  adventure in the necessary re-identification
  of nebulous uncles cousins and fathers
  —and no less newly delineated was Sam
  the owner, his scarred trunk straddling
  the circle's perimeter
  when store business failed to threaten.

Retrospectively
Sam Greene crumbs all illusions connected
with his species of hobbler and old city cave-dweller
—for anyone I know, certainly for me
he had no words wise or other, no secrets
no expressed or implied regrets
no skeletons or ghosts save one, though it was Sam
and Sam only who remained in the intervals following
the ablutions of each game and each departure of the men,
only he to whom the darkness and its urinous diffusions
formed a complete and never-changing world,
a world intact with its own single sun moon and star
all in one.

    Unshocking and unshaming,
    not even one good hearty laugh was Sam Greene,
    barrelbottom of a storekeeper
    keeping his store and what lay in it
    —who lived alone and alone lived out
    that final segment of his life, framed
    in a three-limbed existence
    with a meaning no more real than the phantasm
    of his right leg.

Before I left
I sought for explanations beyond the bottoms of iced bins,
beyond the curved emptiness in dusty showcases,
beyond the silence once one pale light
dangling from some distant umbilicus
above a flat greenish earth.

    He died unacquitted.

Though I awaited new evidence
no hidden fortune was found in his walls.

GONE

So he lies
Surrounded by a hospital
The big priest
Ukrainian and quiet
(A contradiction in terms)
Towering supine
From white bed-head to foot

Father Zarsky
Big as a church
With his blinking gold tooth
And rich eyes

Who used to squelch a boy's shoulder on sight
With a policeman's hand
And laugh
And break *Joey* into syllables
With "So, JO-EY,
        How's your Momma and your Poppa?" and
        "Are you a good boy?"
So "Fine Father Zarsky fine!"
    "Yes Father Zarsky yes!" in panic
Which was our ritual.

Though he led prayer out of my sight
I watched him take giant steps down my Wesley Street
Collaring his scattered people in their language

And he would drive
His cassock-black Studebaker down Victoria Rqad
On his way to town, giving lifts
To school-bound hitchhiking sons of parishioners
And friends of sons of parishioners.

But you are not old enough Father,
Get up and give the good sisters a rest,
Get back to your place of business
That singular aging church refracting the Byzantine
In brown shingles.

I only read about you now
And imagine your lying there
The hole in your mattress getting deeper
Its walls steeper
So your familiar force and questions
Fall into silence

Swallowed up
In my own time and distance
I almost wish I weren't so grown
That I cannot offer you my shoulder

I wish you weren't too far away
To take it

And not out of fear
I wish it were fine
And "Yes, Father Zarsky, yes."

THE FLESH

The flesh of the synagogue is peeled and devoured
In the rotting of fire times fire

Flame times flame, worked belowstairs
From an old-fashioned spark, breathes
Itself to corporeality, staggers
And flails across and against first
Walls of parchment—makes the magic of dissolution
Upon books and their letters become hueless

Flame vaults from stone to ceiling
And flame measures the narrowness of the stairs,
All to the drunken meeting above

Mouths suck upon the vestibule, bring
The speckled pots of sputum to mindless boil,
Bring to bursting the swinging door to meet
The consecrated brew of softening silver and sweat

Dry stacks of talliths and yamulkahs rise
As incense into the fire's breath that puckers
And pushes out the dancing stained windows—
And the roof trembles, its spine assuming that
Of the book, shrunken and sucked dry
So walls that hid ancient ribs fall like pages

Light beats against Light as a scroll sputters
Like an angry fuse and House cracks

Fire and Ark and Torah tumble through folds of vapour
Through the body of ribs
Into the hot stone mikvah of basement.

The flesh of the fire is sucked and smothered
In the rotting of synagogue times synagogue

WHERE ARE THEY NOW?

The Lewis Twins, Bobby and Billy,
grime-swarthy like underage steelworkers
and carbon-pencil slick, who sparked
as stars in a Whitney Pier sky,
with their voices and white-faced guitars
when I was eleven—
and who actually lived in the house across the street,
rock-a-bobbing out the rock-a-billy standards
with no fancy licks, just plain heavy strumming
with their speckled picks—
not bad grist for the Giant Kingo Bingo Night mill,
in between cards at the Casino Theatre on Victoria Road,
right next door to the Star,
where seven dollars was top money for singers and clowns?

"They Say I'm Rockin' the Cradle Little Darlin' "
would ring out in rehearsal across my Wesley Street
in crude-sugar harmony, and the little girls would
applaud with their eyes and laughter—
sixteen-year-old Billy with his swaying oiled hair,
and Bobby who, off his guitar, was quieter than Sunday.

When they seemed to disappear one day
rumour started and spread and stayed among us
that the boys had had to go to hospital
to have their heads washed out—
a picture which magnified and multiplied
and gave us more pictures, and satisfied,
since the master voices of Victoria Road and
all points east were really gone.

They popped up at a distance, about a year later,
in a different part of the city, strumming another stage,
then slid back into whatever deeps forever—
and it seemed to the kids that their voices
must have changed, now that their heads were washed out
and clean, and the Twins had probably gone
and put on crackling shirts and grown up
in shame and sinking two-part harmony, in places
we couldn't see or care to know about.

Fame
as I knew it in Whitney Pier
was always like that—great enough
to make us feel cheated when it left, but
never important enough to make us call it
back.

CONFESSION

I have never been inside a church
Never stopped beyond the lowest of weathered steps
Never held more than half an eyeful of
Light diffused by intense colours of
Partitioned bodies arching upon windows

And I do not intend to change
Not now
Not ever
Though ungoverned I am by
The extended rules of the synagogue

I am afraid of what I would find
I am afraid that I would not be impressed
(Though I would want to be) but
Find it all that familiar
Despite corporate icons and pastry-white statues

I would find it too easy to beat time to
The scraping of devout feet
Sway too recognizably to
The bending and gesticulating of white fingers

I would fall into the simple pattern of
The people on their long hard wooden benches
People leaning on only a different idiom and
Also no party to recent great awakening or awareness

Found would be a house of worship with
The required minimum of
Four walls and a vaulted ceiling
Stocked with air from behind old doors
Worked candles and stained silver and brass
The smell of old thumbs and pages
White robes in high places

In suspected corners beards are easily hidden so
I would never be any more sure of these shadows
Than of my own.

REUBEN THE MESSIAH MAKES AN IMPRESSION

I will always remember his desperate eyes:
"Believe in me!" they seemed to say,
"Believe in me and you shall know
A greater calm than you have ever known!"

He made me itchy, that male witch
With those bright and puppy eyes of his
And his woman's mouth; I had to turn away
Else I knew that I would strike him,
If only with the flat of my hand.

When I turned to face him again
He had turned away from me;
I resented the implication but was grateful,
And I felt the calm of my own beliefs.

   (I am not a religious man
   but I resent some exotic
   trying to oil my brain
   with outlandish ideas and schemes)

He mumbled something in my direction,
And I noted an eyrie of old men
Pressing as close to him as they dared,
As if they would devour his words and him.

In response to all of this nonsense I laughed,
Whether at him or with him I am unsure
For he smiled at the noises I made.

He is alright, really;
Man to man there's more sense to be had
Than in the morrow whose baying draws near.

It's too late now.

Even I can feel the pressure of the moment.

WESTMORLAND STREET'S OLD MAN

The old man
one-steps it
   one step slow one step
across a horizon
of sectioned sidewalk
Long over
the bafflement
of frangibility
his cheap cane and legs
take in years
per concrete portion
heedless of cracks
and long broken
mothers' backs
The cold
of frostless dawn
sinks deeper
than the smooth skin
of the wind
and a cautious fog
rolls under
morning feet

His suit-coat
of woven bile
opens ancient vents
to the chill
and the old man
huddles one hand
around
the insipid furnace
of a cigarette
he huffs
at the wind
   one step slow one step
cane barely touching
Each hard white chop
of sidewalk
is a desert
an ice floe
and as he passes
he turns
to his left
spitting
something old
into the gutter
then moving on
   one step slow one step
The cooling phlegm
rides damp leaves
that have found
the street
in the dark
Not out of sight yet
his dissonant pant-legs
move like rust

There is a dream
that might plot
better last days
for the faulted face
the absurdly neat
sediment of hair
But in the always
round eyes
of hustling September
the old man
    one step slow one step
grows only very older

THE HIRED HELP HOTEL INDIAN

The Indian snakes
down the mock-green corridors
mad with drink and age
brandishing his late night
weapon brown and yellow
coming astride a nightmare
baggy pants and shoulderless
shirt.
Too weak for knives
holds his sex in his hands
brown and yellow foolery
balls without jingle or jangle
like empty bells.
No young Indians born anymore.
This one face of crevasses
raped canyon of a mouth
eyes two dead seas
purchased feather jaunty
in his cap brown and yellow
insignia. Fluttering identity
badge of business
novel calling card
though his own tribe ran to war
featherless.

He is posted in the next room
sentry duty in the can
and he pees silently and expertly
down the side of the bowl. Stealth
they used to call it. Neither
break nor wet a twig. No noise
before the kill.
But he issues a night cough.
Another. Little muffled ones.
His consumption. Sound of his
sickness hits infects.
By day he takes out garbage.
Prepares for winter. Haunts
a last-century hotel on its end.
Feathers up the arse stages
a bravura dance for a today
with tomorrow.
Kind sirs have him in a bottle.

"Excuse me malecite cousin
of micmac cousin of abnaki.
Here is a certified
cultural anthropologist entitled
to examine your specimen
record your cough as authentic
indian folk-song
thump your chest with a clean hammer.
Diagnose. Report. Wait.
No actual handling you
understand. Nothing personal
The rules.
There is always a place for you
where it is dry and warm
and history. Stand like so
one leg raised.

No more snaking down
mock-green corridors from room
to room screwing out dead lightbulbs.
I am the hunter.
Mighty with a sharpened quill.
Tracing mores. Deputy
of the humanities. Newshound.
Photohawk.
You tickle my inner ear. Any secrets
you keep are safe with me if
your belly is full of respect. I follow
hunt commit this revealing path to
your lair to memory.
Don't shoot.
Look. Weary warrior you are as safe
as you have ever been.
It snows two inches
day and night
covering my tracks."

CHANGELING

there's life in the old dog yet
they said
and they let him live

kind they were
shoving the old hair out into
the great inspiring bloody Canadian winter

so he wandered on all fours
(that is what he was taught to do)
and he passed many provinces
and many women
and he thought how if he were a man
he would lay them down
not.make love
dogs don't make love

shiver rain fell everywhere he went
and if it wasn't that it was
bright flashing lights coldly
burning out his eyes   and sludge
and when it was dry summer
dust and small stones
and when it was hard winter
ice shot was slung at him
by plowing boots and shoes
then small boys hurled their flinty tears
at him
and he had a hell of a job
unmatting his hair
from all that skinhot effluvia

he moved on

he didn't like the sea he didn't like water
and the wind
wasn't like it was

all that came to his nose now
was feigned sweat
and it made him sick

once in a lonely torn field
he even dodged rural bullets
and he felt like no hero

people he didn't even know took
the time of day to ignore him
in many languages
as he padded through the marshy alley exusia
of citified country

how he longed for a bone
digging digging he had spent all of his life
digging on hard ground

he was saddened by the absence
of familiarity to his nose
at all the accustomed dog places

he learned to seal off his ears to the noise
he was afraid that in time he might understand

it was lonely
for his kind was largely doored off
or educated away from him

he would catch
brief glimpses of fur from time to time
but was never sure of his eyes

he feared a trap

once on a sun day
a brief shoot of cloud
sending a digital shadow over his melty tracks
convinced him
he had a soul
and knowing his number now made it easier
and his last days were spent avoiding
puddles and people

he died all by himself one dawn
in frosty pain
from the years barking jesus

no-one remembered his mother
or who his friends might have been
and they buried him on the prairies
(it was as far as he had gotten)

no-one robbed him
of his name or birthright
he owned neither

as a marker some old breezy wit shoved
a fender from an old Henry J into the earth
over his tail

sweet ball-shaped national plums
grow in a year by where
he was born

DUSTPAN BILL

Had he been content merely to strangle
His sacrificial recruits, Bill would deserve
Less of our sympathy;
But he took the time of the single man
With each of his lovelies, to bury
His clean teeth in the waning heat and little-bird flesh
Of their breasts; a dandy mouthful of pain and beauty
To feed and fuel him, until next the hunger
Rose to knock impatiently against his ribs
And white eyes.

And yet we doff our hats to Bill because
He went so far, and no farther,
Tempered by temporary satiety.
He kindly left them entombed amidst their own
Earthly belongings, charmed
By the mark of one gentle god, a signature
Written with the burning mouth.

He was a nice guy, who certainly did not make it obvious
To those women who could envision themselves surrounded
By him,
That he was more than they were given to know, more
Than he allowed himself to understand.
And with all that travelling between altars,
He brought to each one the one name of knife.

Modest, one who under other laws
Might have been even more generous,
Bill knew he might be called to task
(He was so alone in his work), yet
He flushed with surprise when his call came.

In looking upon his photograph
I can feel a dissipated wave of his shame's hurt.
Such a young and fine-looking, rich-limbed, neat deity;
Who ought to have minded his business better than he did.

Bill, they will say you are crazy
And all sorts of mad things about you; all things
Born in the fresh-smelling logic of discovery.
Things that had no shape yesterday, but once spoken
Will probably be true enough tomorrow.

A MINOR SPARROW

Only yesterday I saw two
Boys (minus stetsons, neckerchiefs & khaki shorts) pick
A tumbled young sparrow from the rough
Sidewalk, and toss it with flair and success to
The roof of a bystanding verandah.

Today I passed the same way and looked
Up to see the bird, its legs perfunctory breeze-ridden
Stems, lying exact and dead.

Only a damn fool like me would attempt to follow up
Such items, would award continuity to that which
A variegated humanity has already pressed away
Between the scrapbook covers of night and day.

What a gilt-remover for the ornate
Deeds that are done,
This!
>   Clean windows are begrimed,
>   Cut grass grows,

>   And now I wonder what eventually happens
>   To all those old ladies helped across the streets.

WHICH

Jittering chicken
                    and
    Wabbling egg

Both
        beat it down the road
        To the finish line

Egg was first by a feather

THE COLOURS

Before flying to London
   I must visit
   some downtown Fredericton hardware store
   and invest
   in a couple of modest but distinguishable nylon
   Canadian flags to sew upon my baggage
   and shoulders

Without them
   Europeans will feel
   that I have to be
   American

And that
   just isn't close
   enough

IN MY STUFFED CANADIAN HEAD

Not once while I was in Britain
   Did the Queen invite me round—
      Not once, though I gave her island my summer

Did she give me the satisfaction of proclaiming
   "Yes Ma'am, I'm a Canadian over here first time!"
   Identification of self I find ill-fitting at home.

But Jim R. Sholl now—licencee, hence
   Landlord of the King's Arms pub in Eccleshall—
      Master of a second wife who, with her thick right heel
         Cracked the cast for landlord's wives as she stepped out—

Welcomes and warms me with his holy whisky and blessed bitter,
   Into a rain-forest of suspended mugs and refracting light,
      Well past the hour of legal propriety, his beamish handlebar
         Aglisten and curling with illicit goodwill—

Makes my head a washpot of wartime tales—tales of Moncton
   Canada, in the years preceding my infant slathering,
      And how the French girls there would lift their terrible noses
         To destroy the waifish British boys in and out of uniform.

And Jim assures me that sundry little Jims were left there
   To sprout—as legacy, reaffirmation, proof of purchase,
      Sane accidents of the time. Says Jim
         "By God I must have had fun—look at me now!"

I try, and right enough Father Jim stands on my side
    Of the bar—the most important voice and sweat among
        All these voices and sweats, insisting that By God
            I return one eve for another and another.

Little jims and crusts of War in Canada
    Flob in jello behind my eyes—little jims
        Beginning to do sodden battle among themselves
            In my stuffed Canadian head.

So and now Mrs. Jim is out here too with us,
    Her own and wonderful perfume spilling
        Like beer over the brim, through the starry pub
            Over all the premises and players.

I am hugged to her bosom—I cling there,
    An ant to the precipice. I am kissed out the door
        With all the regal weight and splendour
            Of a Midland landlord's Welsh-veined wife.

Now there was Welcome—a Welcome no longer,
    But a well-orbed haunting of fullness
        In the heart's warm belly.

AN END TO AN END

Afterimage to all eulogies for Robert Francis Kennedy, Autumn 1968

As long as we are moving in black
so long as we become mourning as it becomes us

why not crank out an alkaline tear and more
for the other dead

for the indecently stepped-upon sports fans
of a sweaty latin soccer game

for the lead-lined confusions
basted in distant paddy water

for the never-never-to-be doctors
lawyers and cattle thieves   shot
beaten and victimized by road misadventure
the world over

for Mr. Tinker and Mrs. Tailor who lost out
on a Pre-Judgment Day claim to fame
through the democratic law of Supply and Demand

for the pill-stopped knots of unmatter
never to rotisserate and come womb-sliding

Let us each pay homage to them all
by becoming scatterers of pollen-laden memorials
in their honour

exercising our communicative organs
as aeon-proof cornerstones and pillars
of the edifice Dedicated to Universal Ills

as breathing naked monuments
from Beginning to Beginning

Savour it
our effigial selves in a World Park
where existence will be Meaningful

and all we need fear
are the thousand-year rain
and the pigeons

KISS

in
wet
caves

worm
is
met
by
worm

slither

head
to
root

a
rumbling
of
entrances

bloody
avalanche

FOR NOTES TOWARD A JEWISH POEM

I trust
      in the fundamental—
   chart the rising and falling
   tide of the patriarchs breaking
   within me

this far inland
   from the moon.

THE READING

I've watched them all, some of them friends
—they've written and played their words out
into and against the familiar spectator wall
And a bad poem makes noises like a flat tire

Now see this one "offstage" suffering
the wait for introduction, presentation
to this bunch—then
the mutual tasting

Again and again they are too young and too old,
convinced only in percentage of any godhead
present—Poetry with any dual nature

They are somewhere beneath him, yet my friend
quivers, quakes, sweats to fill his boots
He has premonitions of artistic failure,
of a not-so-artistic destruction
His bowels give a constant cry for attention,
for the "at ease" stance, as he fills the washroom
they provide—expecting the other call,
leaning tightly over the basin

I wait
within its mirror

I know whence come the hunter and the sailor
But from where does the poet come
that he arrives at
this.

TRUTHS BEING FLOWERS

For Barbara

Truths being flowers
I pin this bud to your shoulder
no orchid or sweetheart rose it

rides with the rider
just as exposed
as the teller

may he strum the fine earth
might this lifegiver gardener
turn out others

Truths being flowers
I eliminate the shops
bring this straight to white shoulder
fix it there with warm fingers

this one flower
there are no more
though I do anything good
there are no more

give it no rain
but your breath
that there be full opening
and discover that

in your moist darkness
it stays   so many
you need both hands
to count it

SHADES

It is May
  with no pole

yet nine children
            (little girls by the look of them)
  make and maintain the perfect circlet
    dresses hooping like the dresses of old
      genuine pigtails in flight
hands dancing

  on a school green somewhere
    in outer Saint John

Something to watch   this
from a distance
in a moving car

  The circle is still very much alive
as we drive deeper into the city
where the same shape dancing
  is performed with questionable purpose

ANOTHER "ROAD MOVIE" (1942-43)

If we'd been alive
then   there—
I would probably have lived long
enough to regret it
                    And us

I'd doubtless have wound up
a sorry stain in a forcibly unclean
bottom layer   on one last relentless train
    with fear in every part but its engine
And me envious but terrified
of all the rising steam
and carelessly sloughed smoke

If we could have known one another
then   I would have tried to stomach all
that certainty   disbelief and horror
And excrete at least a limp diarrhetic passion
for you

With everything out of control
I would probably (at a risk to us both) have tried
to hold on to you
                    All one of the foolish chosen
could ever do for another

And you? Despite our separate streams
and your father the Schutzstaffel monster
    you   I believe
would have cried

A SHORT HISTORY

I was not always a poet
enraged by other poets
but was once a fisherman
who, catching no fish

played with a knife
while my father caught a fish
that was no poem
when I had got through with it.

DEALINGS WITH GRANDEUR
OF A SATURDAY AFTERNOON

More than anything else
  At this moment I want to be
    Inspired like the apple-veined
      Others who sat great heads nodding
     In ritual recall of genius before
    A brew of colours or keyboard
     Of ivory and ineffable letters

    My curtains are torn
   Open the sun set to streaming past
  My work and I poised with my machine
 In a balance of air arced upon
A thick wall of permanence

  While across the fat alley
   A small bored blonde turns
    To ask passing men
     If they are
      Drunk

FAMILIA IN EXTREMIS

I lay my trust in the cosmic serenity
of budded mothers—all impregnated women
have that look about them
a control as strong as quiet
that says:

        I am being kicked and punched
        and bitten by growth
        and generally tested by this
        ex-seed that holds me
        responsible and O planter
        you came in and left in a flash
        of no more or less than flesh
        mere as mine though less dead
        than our hair and nails

Let us say
that a man begins in pain
and ends in pain
and at places in between
causes a great deal of it
in his childish manipulation of creation

He hurts and cries out
while only a woman endures
which a woman enjoys for its rights
and is designed for
which is why eyes and smiles
of real children are bound only to her
eyes and smile
all with the instinct of more than a cat

Primed with raw stuff and catalyst
she generates bone and fibre within
a setting gelatin to glisten and be weaned
slowly on an emulsion and the low flame
of their wetted oneness

Rude red progeny is hers
now to hold and hold into shape
with the only genuine passion
and that which lies between mother and child
lies deeper than any thing between any other
(no man ever shining wet enough to win
entrance to the deepest vitals)

Nothing comes from a man's belly to compare
but you must go down to his underground
sustaining stream—all an abstract
to a child who is for years
an abstract to itself

The child and his lady
madonna and child—
the insidious potentialities

Note:
        their conviction and fear perhaps
        right perhaps half right and worthy
        of some consideration
        that the male of the species
        alone in genetic anger and hunger
        and given the opportunity—
eats his children

LE MASQUE FINIS

A while ago
           a square bottle of wine
cut an ache
in our throats
         Now
with you asleep on our argument
                  its remainder
a sour lukewarm phlegm
rides the hind of my gullet
like a small mean child

The stickiness of loving is unstuck and timed
by the travelling clock

I am up
        painting your room with my eyes
the Chagall poster the Eskimo print
            Don Quixote
The distended shelves the corners
sandals indented with the damp weight of you
the orange rug with the bug I killed in your honour

The kitchen
      cold
I embrace a wine-glass half-filled with orange juice
I might have been swimming in some heavy sea for this thirst

Down
      comes the thermostat in the close other room
Several of your poster sketches have slipped their taping
and slid in an electrostatic manner
along the panelled wall to the floor
                                    I look
and am surprised
                  They covered nothing
No scratches or nail holes
                            no peeling beneath the peeling

You hid nothing really

An evening of exposures
                        and I am better off outside
where I realize that the wind
which usually blows from the moon
                                  does not quite reach
tonight
      I suppose it is the season

Inside you probably sleep without your anger
                                          now
while the stars I can identify
                              do not just flicker
They almost glare and burn
                          at me
like the little suns they are.

I HAVE JUST COME IN FROM A RUN IN THE RAIN

I have just come in from a run in the rain
And though this girl at eight and this boy
at eleven and I are bloodbound
it has not shown much
during this my visit to the town of our birth

smiles and speeches wanting and insufficient
and because I am 23 and a man
I cannot coddle them or play to them

I have grown awkward without brothers
and sisters
I have forgotten how little
girls can be

This rain now
finding us on our return from the park
catching us in the wide open and we run
I not too fast for her running (as she
likes to put it) between the drops

the girl sketching a pattern
of healthy giggles, her country brown hair
flying and falling under
the positive pull of drops to her face

our feet lifting up and carrying
tracers of fallen rain and wet
earth to our legs

The boy pushes through
the motions of running on his two-wheeler
and we make the jokes he is made of
Me wondering if he knows why he rides
his bicycle where he does

I am taken in by this weather

Rain that pierces but is not fatal
I had forgotten
what this kind of wetness was like

We interrupt wherever
trees and their branches come together
for cover

With no-one else around we laugh a lot
I more than what I've grown used to

In the shadow of the rain everything
green is greener and there is
much of it yet in this town
light around and up

The streets are wet with life

This is our grandfather's house
here
Is it as large
are the hills as steep
to them as they were to me

This now their home is old and firm
enough to muffle the sound of the rain

As we climb stairs to the verandah the girl
takes and holds my hand
till we are inside
just like that
                    I say nothing
and if I am wise
I will never question her

I feel very fine thanks
and explicably important
Important as these two
whom I'd not seen for eight years

Not to hurry
the change to dry clothes
Paul laughs and Esther says "Let's
wait until just before supper"

This is summer

We are warm

We will dry before tomorrow

when the bus is to pull me away
again as before
and introduce me to the other lives
I live
and their devices

So now may the three of us track in the rain
through the rooms of the family

The gods of the afternoon and I
are at home.

LOVE POEM DE HABANA

I cannot write about your favour of breasts
    Or your eyes which bruise their wings against me
Or your body which improves my bed
    Or your head which graces my armpit
Or your fingers which impress my body
    Or your sleep which pulls you to me
Or your anger which rattles chains

    I cannot write about them
    Because they are too near
    And I have you

Rather let me pay paper court
To your female acquaintances
    The ones in whom I can descry streets and buildings
The ones my eyes can follow
With their fisted greed

    For they are the ones I will not have
    As I have never had them
    Nor do I want them
    For I would then have even fewer poems
    And you would have only their company

Let them open the gates for my eyes
    Let my eyes beget tongues
Let these celebrate your birthday at their party
    Let their vitals be content with prose

Welcome me home from my compulsive rag-picking
With your lust and your love and no mirror

    And thus do I ask of you
    Choose your friends carefully

POEMS FOR MY UNBORN CHILD

I

I cupped my right palm
over your shape
and felt you
tonight

(it was too dark
for me to know
which side of you
it was I touched)

are you too young to know
someone was there?

you slept then
for us and for yourself

and though your face
could not yet be seen
it was in your mother's
I looked for and found you

Ann heard your voice
yesterday evening
(your heart so little
so big) mysterious
and unmindful of sex

heard it through the magic
of an amplified stethoscope

(knowing it's there's just knowing it

hearing it's touching it
knowing it)

will you hide from us?

for how much longer?

3

A life
discovered here
frail as any
and whole

between the lid-thumping thrub
in your first contralto
and the heavier song
above it

4

Diminutive semiticelt
horseshoe of life

you breathe already
in such a way
as to send fish scurrying
to an unexplored sea

little fish yourself
kicking when we forget
and consider ourselves

with a whale's cry of loneliness
going nearly unheeded
lost
in the throat-parching ocean

its beaches
the rind of your world

5

Nothing
between you and me
now
but both sides of flesh
and the First Age of Pain

THE LITTLE JOKE

Ahh!
       she cried and broke
Ahhh!
         her disparate parts trembling she cried
I cannot mother!
How dare they!
               and she let rage in to heat her tears
to scalding.
They tell me I cannot feed my child,
my first child, my only child;
my breasts so large and golden, the two
so heavy for him and ah! they forbid me
to place their buds in his mouth,
they deprive me of my pleasure; they would
give him bottles and the stinking rubber;
witches' teats!
Lord when mine are so ready!
Why do they hate me?
Her husband, his bones and flesh apart, paced accordingly. Wiped
her tears and his sweat from off his face, wiped the acids upon
his poor sleeves. He bobbed for her in a tried movement and she
pushed him away. With her wet hands. And he felt old and useless,
alien and lost.
I know you!
         his brain cried at him, as the rest of him
reeled in several directions.
My love!
        said his mouth,
Please don't worry and fret.
Please don't cry so.
O if I could help, my dearest!
You are still his only mother,
his mother, pet, as always you were.
We shall feed him together.

Look!

        and in anticipation of a little joke, his moustache
wiggled its ends, wiggled its whiskertips. Like a child's ears
or an old man's eyebrows.

  Now if I was like that Bible chappie
  —darn him dearie what was his name—
  the one who had to handle this newborn babe,
  a godgiven child, so who asked the Lord to help,
  and upon whom God caused to grow a real pair
  of woman's knockers;
                       (he was laughing outright now)
  why if I had those
                 (and here he puffed up his little chest)
  or even one,
  real bazoomers with real nipples don't you know,
  I could feed our child meself now couldn't I,
  and you wouldn't have to worry but would
  look at me the two of you together lovey
  eh?

Simply bemused now, his thin low chuckles riding and sliding and
slipping in her tears, over her long hair and body, he reached down
to touch her and was again rebuffed. This time for good.

She paused a sweep's moment only before resuming the keening
deep in her practised throat, her laden breasts shaking at the start
of the swing, then swaying as she rose up—flowers grieving to
burst with bloom or die—

  Ahh!

     (it came)

  Ahhh!

     (she breathed and broke again).

FACES

1

This legion of faces
made by my seven-week-
old daughter Rebekah

are as those made
by some wise and ancient
lady
who has not all that suddenly

realized
that what she is seeing is
in fact only temporary

2

Rebekah you are
    a veritable gargoyle
your womb-cut tongue
    a trough   a drainway
for the unswum sky
    And as the stone nest
of your hinged face
    takes shapes of change
it is at once
    the frieze of movement
round the perimeter
    of a high cathedral
or other holy edifice
    The sounds you make
are those anyone can hear
    who takes his life
into fingerpads and feet
    and climbs to join you
perched there
    on the edge

NOT THE HORNED FLESH

A cappella for Ann

I set the words *I Love You*
In, and recite them to you
Nearly as gracefully as when
First I ingested their consequence.

I recall them for you
                              —companions to the satyr's pledge
                              of hand upon knee
—where majuscule and minuscule
conjoin with the stews
                              —even as you hunch in prayer
                              over your alchemicals
—while you juggle your breasts and hair
before the dancer in the glass.

My words are your tenacious company
—that I might never regret their unsaying
—that they might buffer the moments of word-harm
—that what is eventually defaced might not go unprefaced
And that the graceful cat in you might lick its whiskers
Clear of cream.

My axiom, each word is an extension of the flesh.
Each word is as finger; rare-formed, vein-proud, gentle;
Not without its horn of nail,
For such would be hideous and alien.
But with its mooned edge clipped clean.

And as with other fingers on another hand,
The semitic blades extending seconds past the tubes of flesh;
A measure to create pleasure-circles upon your back
As you huddle in the tub, like a child conscious
She is a burlesque of the foetus;
Or when you lie in our bed on your side as a woman
And watch away, to see whatever shades are summoned
By my cabbalistic rune-scratch.

Such nexus exists without ardour;
It is the wee girl in you once more,
The nude remnant of a waif, who begs
For this larger hand to animate, "Yes Please."

And you always request that bit of the nail
Laid on, not too deep but deep enough to scratch,
To leave tracks, to give evidence of that game
—the touching of old gods—
Before the writing goes inside.

I Love You
   Having once brushed them,
   It is the words
      —Not the horned flesh—
  Shall lift your bones
  To my surface.

MEMORIAL SERVICE FOR THE LIVING (1969)

My grandfather is alive   81
and recovered from the operation
that sent him   nearly took him completely
away from his family   who all knew
he would die   (my mother, her brother
and sister, my father, my grandfather himself
and his remaining old friends, me)

He left us   shaking
our hands   wet face already turned
too far inward toward his knotted belly
   his suit hanging upon him   so much weight

It's his constitution   his sister said
The family constitution that held him   holds him
64 years from Kimkowich   near-cancerous
miles from Latvia   proof of a wonderful constitution
that would in a dance with malignity stammer
his going with sharp swirls of pain

I admit to having prayed for him
as I once had to pray for my father   mumbling
a stumble of words   uncomfortable repeating
that unnameable name of a god
that He   so indecisive   might hear

I said *God help him* over and over
   I was obligated to pray   obligated
by habit and heritage as lasting and as binding
as scrolls   obligated through fear   grey shame
   assumed guilt

And so

I said *Help him God*   not
Let him live   not *Preserve him*
but whatever's best (no suffering on my account
or on the account of all those misguided
and related by blood)

I don't know what I meant when I spoke
     never enough   death-distant   annoyed
and awkward   all sentiment skimmed away
by every sort of gathered distance

I make no excuses
I know that on my own first turn toward death
I will want my people praying for me
     no taking of chances   no harm in praying
like hell   And not just anything
And nothing ambiguous
please

I will want my people to say much   mean more
than simply to help me
They must find the height and master
of some heaven   words to get within
     words of praise and panic   words
that will require my long life to live out
their promises

Surely my grandfather prayed for himself
as I will for myself   as I will have to
For no-one can say what I will say
or do what I must do
in that most religious babble.

ADDITIONAL SERVICE: THE ANNIVERSARY

(I had one uncle once
and he was a better man than I
though he had not the sum of my duties,
and he was a lesser man than I
though he had not the sum of my shortcomings.
While I was young enough
still to colour my dreams of God with his face and frame,
he would ofttimes wink at me; our confidence
that only I cared about.

           When I grew tall enough
to stand head-to-head with vanity,
           inefficacy,
           self-pity,
he let me go.

         As his sight and other senses withered
mine grew more knowing; he was in the position of a man
straining to see, yet
straining to be unseen
at once.
        And he hid only from himself.
        And it killed our confidence.

My father, you see, was dead
before I could smile knowingly at him; so
I gave his smiles to my uncle.
           And he took them.

And he may have consumed them,
may have rejected them; I may have dreamed
he took them,
for all I will ever know,
for all he will ever tell me.

But our shadows had once been twins in promise,
and he loved something,
and he haunts me yet; for I have plunged deep
into the pool of shadows
and surfaced,
bearing the name
our people gave to him)

This is your death-day my uncle my name
which your children will not remember
for they too are dead

There was a time
when you were caught
in the long worn folds of your life

but your brother had one son
and I am your name and your poor chronicler
and this is your death-day

You were a slaughterer too though no rabbi
                              no cantor
                              no beadle

A slaughterer born
you called yourself
                    bitter

and for all your years
you resisted all presences
especially your own

Your enemies threw jokes at you
A Hidden Saint they called you
(one of the Thirty-Six resting in God's radiance)
because sainthood would have to have been well hidden
under your clump of beard and temper
   (Under what should a saint hide?)

Because you were poor
          you were quiet
Because you were deaf
          you were poor
Because you were quiet
          you smouldered

A child's hand's teeth would comb your beard for feathers
A child's eye's wonder would explore your eyes
and be bruised by the black and the anger

You swept one son from your knee
and called him a man before his time
to be rid of the child

You could not hear his crying
or know that he marked it down
for the chronicles

Your wife called herself
                    sorrow
and we all know what was done to her

how she bore the attack of your eyes and empty hands
and the way they hounded your Sabbath guests
until their shadows ceased to shape the flame blade
                    of the Bride's candles

In the synagogue
your figure twisted at prayers
though your lips remained shut

As you were tricked into sainthood
so some believed you were wiser than you evidenced
but where did you keep your books and your love?

Your sons were shot my uncle
and you must have mourned silently
    Your wife left and you again voiced no thoughts

    When you died you were alone and free of tricksters
    Were you silent?
I am your name and your chronicler

    (When such a saint has children
what are the children of saints?)

    A child who is not your child asks of anyone
one last question
as yet unanswered by the sages and tellers of tales:
    Can a Hidden Saint truly be hidden
even from himself?

CHAIM THE SLAUGHTERER

I

One of the children is frightened of me
because his father permitted him
to stand and watch
last week's ritual slaughter.

I will remember the face
I saw when I lifted my eyes from my work—
    it was frozen in the sensation of knife
    wet at the end of my arm.

And because I understood his desire
to come nearer, I smiled, for
I so rarely have a witness
of whom I am aware.

But the scab-pools of blood upon my hands
drove him away, as did that blood
yet to be fully drawn into the earth.
And perhaps my smile.

I interest him now
only through his fear. Thus
my tongue can but fail with this boy of seven,
though he has been taught
the necessity of koshering.

I might try and tell him
what I myself sometimes believe:
that the hands of this slaughterer and the hands of this rabbi
are not two and the same
—that in the eye of our God
they are as two and two—each pair
bound to their respective duties.
And that duty is all
they hold in common.

But I know these children—
when this one enters my home (as he must)
to study the aleph-bayz,
to mouth rigid prayers softly
with this teacher and the moist broad thumb that turns
    pages—
he will not rest
until he has again found
my other hands.

2

I have just now paid the Gentile boy
who enters our synagogue once each week
to kindle the fires for Sabbath morning
services.

This costs the congregation 25 cents.

In Latvia
such a sum would have lasted months of the Pentateuch—
in fact
a pinch of Sabbath cake was often enough
reward.

But I have no heart for reminding the boy
how brief and simple his duties are;
nor do I wish him to feel that his job is not
important.

So I pay him the 25 cents.

All this morning I have stood here,
bowing against the flatness of my feet,
slicing with my hands
                  under feather, through
                  fat and flesh and vein,
many necks.

The men force the odoriferous mouths of chicken sacks
under my beard—I turn my face, dip
my arm to its shoulder to fill my hand
with noise and yellow claw.
All this morning.

And there is a sun which, heavy, seizes
and twists the blades of my shoulders
           the blade in my hand
           the blade in my head.

My hearing is rotten with complaint, my eyes
are filled with hot wax, and beard and dust
are in my mouth
tasting of what dances and splutters in the yard.
My sweat thins their blood
                  —salt to mix with salt.

I sway
      almost
stumble
        into the east.

O Men (I think),
put away your sacks filled past their stinking brims!
You have more than enough to barter,
to eat—
        I
        myself
        have already feasted
                far beyond my fill.

Late in the afternoon
I found our small Gentile boy
(who can be no more than twelve)
between the worn covers of a Sabbath prayer-book,
deep in the corner of the synagogue basement.

He had been about his normal duties when I left;
and I returned, to stand mute and well away
from the court of sunlight and the student's desk,
both of which he occupied
—neither of us alert to time.

Upon his finally discovering me
he released the Hebrew book
and arose quickly—his face tight and red
                    like an accomplished fist,
                    his freckles thus obscured.

I lifted up the Siddur myself and saw
that his eyes had been at the familiar
prayers of the morning service,
but this child had been holding them
upside down.

A smile refused to stay behind my nod of sanction,
and an alien explaining tongue babbled past my smile.

A solemn form
moved its shadow over mine and across the threshold
    of the place—

it was then
            I heard the boy laugh.

I have performed this act so many times
   that my body is shaped to suit the knife

Each bird is the same in my head
   whatever differences found in the yard

Held for events by an alien hand
   each bird I hold is raggish
      squirming only its heart under feathers and fat

Each bird stifles itself senseless
   uneasy off the ground
      where these wings could never carry it

Legs and breast are tucked in my left arm
   while the other cradles the glinting refrain
      of all such mornings

There is a noise which is shaped in its throat
   and held in the throat as a weapon
      and it is that throat I must find

One hand settles a stuttering head
   and free fingers draw the down
      from its womanish neck

I fold my arms across pulse and breath
   where a noise is soft
      where nothing resists

Almost
   I can believe
      it is the chicken which slides into the knife.

6

She is a rebbitzen:
                    wife of an orthodox rabbi
                    assistant to an orthodox teacher
                    companion to an orthodox slaughterer.

When she was a maiden
she was also a butterfly (and called so by her sister and
                                        mother and
                                        father).

When she first became what she is
she had of necessity to shave her head
and wear a wig, to cover her arms and legs
with dark sleeves and skirts.

A butterfly.

A rabbi must show no interest
in a woman, even his wife.
It is forbidden.
His wife is functional
and has no reason to flaunt her body,
as her husband may not look at her with lust.
Such
is the law and obedience—

for in those different years
in that different country
I obeyed fully
and my wife was always dutiful
as required.
On this
as on few other matters
she said nothing.

The years and I have worn
against each other,
and I take and allow to be taken
great leniencies
—many more than I should.
Many more.

This is a strange country and a trying one, though
I make no excuses.

So, somewhere
my wife received my silent permission
to grow and care for her hair;
for some years now
she has been wearing dresses with shorter sleeves,
dresses that reveal the backs of her knees
(On some of these are painted
butterflies.)

She is nearly bald; one might count
the remaining wisps,
and while none are so white
as hairs in my beard, they are
at least grey.
             She must wear a wig.
Her arms are unsightly with fat (and yellow
like old sour cream). She ought to wear sleeves.
Her legs are weathered pillars.
Sweat collects quickly
in the rills of her neck.

What can I tell her that she cannot tell herself?
I consider:
             the cruelties of time
             the ironies of mind
             and place
                  and time... (flying and crawling backward)

But I do not complain.

On this
as on few other matters
she says nothing.

A moment ago I lowered my eyes
from the slashing of throats to the earth
—never before have I seen so much blood
atop the ground.

As a rule, the run of a single morning is small,
and the blood (save that which clings to the kaftan,
my blade and fingers) is swallowed by the earth
without question.

There is always a spotting from the chicken's efforts, but
today a red pool has grown
from the earth's refusal—at my feet.
I cannot understand it.

   (So little from each one;
   so many there must have been
   passed between my hands.)

There are no children.
I have no son, no daughter

In 36 years
she and I have lived
as fellow travellers on a train might
share the same bench for a long journey,
who while never really knowing each
the other, will yet experience
a distinct feeling of loss
upon the inevitable hissing arrival
at journey's end.
Any degree of familiarity carves
deeply into any relationship—
but the travellers are unable
to explain such strange needs
for one another.

I am never unaware
of the presence of my wife.

(How may a man be unique and still a mortal? Is a man who
accepts a life in the shadow of God's books a man?)

There was a brief moment when seed
took root, took nourishment and grew—
there was a season.
And what has happened since
is decreed
no more. A piece of wood has no recollection
of its earlier life, of what
once fell from its branches.
Love, hatred, anger, passion—in what
does any of it ever result? A child
is either a moon's revolution in the life of man,
or a creature unto itself.
I have observed children.

What can I say of mothers,
of their unassailable unctuous place
in the eye of God?
While to sire
is but to place a sweating unreasoning self
in the dry palm of a God at work.

Less and less often
does my oval mind reflect
upon its flesh reincarnate
over the bone carriage, created
through no art of mine.

My wife and I have no son,
no daughter.
There are no children.

9

Alone in the sweatbath
   I am truly a naked bather

  alone with all that is
    in me on me and about me.

This shvitzbud with its water forms
   has a hollow that wants filling

  and surrounding the hollow
    is the stone.

My naked arm strains at the iron lace
   of the faucet's red wheel

  to set forth a torrent which is noise
    and another wall.

Echoes of my movements intertwine in passing
   to form a quilt for my senses

  as I give myself up
    to the water and its mists.

I have prayers to tell to the stone
   and dusts of book and yard to wash away

  and the feather seeds need weeding
    from my beard.

The stone and I are worn and yellow
   yet standing

  and naked
    I am truly ageless.

My feet (of necessity) clutch
   the very stone the rest of my body repels

  but the innate coldness of that touch
    is a purgative come early.

I sing songs of battle and children
    to frighten away the spirits

        who seek out any orifice I own
            to enter.

I sing songs of children and praise
    and I am an ancient army

        passing through some ancient sea
            that obeys me.

I am a child
    with a child's sensations

        and the noise of God's names
            rebounds and redoubles.

God's names are thrown from stone to stone
    stone to water

        but though they eat their own intensity
            the sound does not leave this place.

Something
    joins me in this chairless room

        that is barely large enough
            for me.

When I leave my cavern
    I am weak with loss and gain

        and far from naked
            and prepared to topple.

I wonder at the secret qualities of my blade
that cause it to withstand the stain of its work.

Would that there were something in me
that could help me to withstand the stains of my own life

or something or someone that might wash for all time such
stains from this shaft   my person.

Would that there were no blade
to cleanse.

I wind the phylacteries close about me
> —a bandage
> —a ribbon
> —a vine

And it shall be unto thee for a sign
  upon thy hand

   My left arm is one foundation
on which is wound this reminder of our God
whose leather temple rides my sinews
> rides nearest the seat of my faith

   The road from this temple is spiral wonder
which helix coils as black bone seven times
my arm to my wrist
and its welt likewise marks my palm
   God is bound to my median finger
> wound thrice

and extended
> aiming

at the wordless marrow of my devotions

And for a memorial
  between thy eyes

   The twin black temple rests upon the foundation of my
     forehead
is looped and knotted
   Exodus and Deuteronomy are tossed thus by prayer
> prayer which

   rids and replaces
the passion that is the corruption
> the corruption that enslaves

heart and mind

In order that the law of the Lord may be
  in thy mouth

    Had I only my right arm
I would of necessity use it
                        wound tight through another's
    assistance
    Had I suddenly
no arms
          the covenant would remain
                            spoken and unspoken
with the ghost of my arm
responding
to the fact of the pressure
closing
upon it

For with a strong hand
  hath the Lord brought thee forth out of Egypt.

12

Blood flows like water from a nurturing fountain

Solemn but godly beauty flows through the necessity
   of the flow

Amidst such
                     on this poor and sticky morning
these
creatures (having no more respect or knowledge
   of their lives than God gave them)
make not even
the necessary
noises.

13

Today
a child of my congregation asked me
why my back is bent when I walk.

                              Now
I am afraid to know that she is right,
for I was not aware that I had become stooped.
It does not surprise me.

The ground seems as close to me as it has always been.

14

I am told that some of the names I am called
are terrible—as terrible as any I have ever heard
and understood.

These people
are difficult to comprehend.

They will also insist on shouting at me
                              "Jew! Jew!"
and I answer them in Yiddish
                              "Of course I am, idiots—
and what might this slaughterer's knife
(which I carry in its black case) have to say to you,
were I not
such
a Jew?"

15

They
yell at me
        "Santa Claus give us a present!"
        "Santa Claus where are your reindeer?"
        "Santa Claus why is your nose so red?"

They laugh and gesticulate and dance about as if possessed
   of dybbuks.

My Yiddish goes no farther with them
than my beard.
What I say is
        "I am sorry.
You must have confused me with someone
else."

16

When an unclean chicken dies
its worms and lice die
soon after.

This seems neither good nor bad
                  but
sometimes
        before I can expel the damned carcass
the vermin light upon my arms
and (against the wish of God) I feel
that I must crush their hardnesses with my nail
—I must be convinced in the silences between my fingers

that they might not doom me too
as their host.

17

This knife
        which must be prepared,
        which must be clean to cut clean,
        to take and give without waste
        in that guttural rite with any selected animal
           (save the unclean 42)
—

can be wielded by no other,
exercised for purpose

none other than this.

Yet
      if this knife
      were made ready
      and proffered
      for any other act of will
        (to some incredible blasphemer)
—

who could take it
and use it
now?

18

As an artless young student
I often dreamt shapeless dreams
about conducting forth my people
to Eretz Yisroel, our Promised Land.

Now, upon these ritualized legs
I lead a congregation of strangers
around the long floor of the synagogue;

while familiar voices, shouting
from out a brilliant doorway,
own to the youngest having left
(for some nearer wayside) even this
reminder of tribes.

19

The birthday of the world begins
The Ten Days of Penitence

The Days of Awe
when the rabbis lead the multitude
past the Heavenly Throne and the eye of God

with our hearts opened
to Him
who needs no opening:

We are the contents
of the Book of Life
    the Book of the Dead
and between

We feast throughout our joyous solemnity
and give thanks for our being sustained
to this day
            An apple dipped in honey is the year to come

    The Days of Awe
are the days of flooding sins
against Man
against God

Each asks forgiveness of each
Each grants forgiveness to each
until God alone is left
the Day of Atonement

Washed clean of earthly transgressions
we in our bathwater
now ask forgiveness
for those who have reached out to sin

In pious white we take no food
but prayers
We chew on prayers to the fifty-sixth genus of sins
and spit them out

We cry and atone
even for those sins
which are not meant
to be sins

   My knees fail
and my tears fall
as my prayers touch
the Ineffable Name

When the sun gives way
to little suns
   loud voices
proclaim the Oneness—

      It is the wail of the ram's horn
      that calls us away
      from our whiteness

      and chills the demon bones
      of Satan and his hosts
      who await our coming forth—

         At length
         when the doors of the synagogue
         are locked behind me

         I do not wonder
         at the black winds
         that scratch at my old clothes

         or the leering faces
         that beg my reacquaintance.

20

I have need of a new stylus,
a pointer—
the one I now use and have been using for years
is broken.
> A shaped stick of insignificant metal
> looking like no man's arm,
> it ends in a tiny hand balled
> but for one finger cast in the act of pointing;
> but this finger is severed at the knuckle
> and lost.
My pointer for our Law is and has for some years now been jagged.

The other ageing elders and I unravel the Torah each Sabbath,
rolling the scroll past each glued pane of parchment, to find the
place and to continue the story from the week before.

(Only these voices could ever have been new)

These men know their job well:
> one pulls
> one pushes
> and the hand-lettered Five Books
> of Moses roll like newsprint.
Hands and handles
beat the table
with an atavistic rhythm—
> my large brown hand
> and the small grey fist
> hover in wait—
upon the line spun from lost finger to line of Law rests
the eye—
> each hand nearly full
> both hands fall like breath
> upon the face of Moses.

At the hinder end of my stylus
which is not silver, is a hole
bored for a single chain or a rich thong—
                              I have neither.

In affluent synagogues
functional ornaments gleam
rich, and nothing is broken
that is not repaired or soon
replaced.
            What matter here?
When Yontiff's Torah is being read, the children
and many men rush to the vestibule to build
upon muffled laughter, fat black cigars,
and the languid dropping
globs of their spit
into the brightest green brass pot.

I conduct the Reading of the Law
to a chorus of distant rumbling,
conjuring up no new emotion in myself,
but with only stale anger sweeping over
those poor prayers of habit, rung from memory.

I conduct the Reading of the Law
with a broken and lost finger,
and a wash of my bile covering
all such prayers.

I chant all
and they rejoice
and trustingly celebrate
all that I chant.

It is no small part of my vocation
to sing from dried skins
lines that are recorded
                        between the lines
                        that have gone and continue to go
                        unrecorded.

21

I am stale.
My beard is stale.
My breath is stale.
My odour (as after sickness) is withering.

Even my wife
shrinks from me.

My congregation
allows itself
to be led
        by a dying man.
            A sick man
shakes hands and (like an ant) leaves a sour smell.

My praying is stale.

I stink of sacrifice.

Give me a new synagogue
            new books
            new scrolls
            new vestments
a new home with a new bed that does not bow lower than its
    occupants.
What do I say? What could I possibly want?
Pummel me into some new shape
and I will remain stale
                worn evenly
                by indifference.
The God of the Jews in my care
is stale to them.
        They are fools
        who have no patience
                no ability to withstand
—children who have not
the excuse of innocence.

I am tired.
I know that my God is tired.

You
tire
him.
You are stale.

His patience is sorely tried.
My hands are helpless. My prayers. . . ?

The road back
is the road
beneath your feet
                    and you claim not to know it.

I am sick from your infection!
                              But you?
Worse than dead
if only you were dead!
                    Will God's worms deign
                    to swallow your eyes?
What have you done to your God
that has fallen on me?

22

How merciful O Lord
    that thou hast given these of your creatures
    such a quick and painless death
    as thou canst afford through my presence

Is it just then that I
    thy manifold servant and one of thy Chosen
    must suffer in this my illness
    when even the lowliest of thy creatures
    is given a death with no dying?

If it is true
    that the Angel of Death wields a knife
    why doth he not use it at once?

I can only conclude
    that thou in thine infinite wisdom
    hast made me a more efficient slaughterer
    than thine other appointed

EPILOGOS

I am standing at the centre of the yard
beneath the morning's familiar   the sun
About me in a ragged ring are men
and some women   their faces known to me
and yet unidentifiable   Their feet and mine
archipelagoes amidst an ocean of dank sawdust
    atop an otherwise denuded earth
Someone hands me a sack busy
with shapeless thrashing   weighted
with life and an ancient smell
My arm makes its forefelt entrance and begins
stretching beyond its capacity   one hirsute tentacle
    through the coarse sack's infinity
and no birds within
It is removed and another is thrust at me   Again
despite all signs there is nothing
and when I look up at the dream faces
they are smiling at me   no   leering
    whatever it is breaking
into the choral laughter of rending parchment
For some reason I accept a third offering
which I refuse to open   though something does tur
and mould fleeting impressions in the cloth walls
Between my heaving rib-cage and my garments
moves a flume of perspiration   Powerful laughter
from the circle of gargoyles washes over me
    with the sun   Each face wrapped
in vicious mockery

But my eyes are drawn to their necks   ropy tendons
framing a soft and pale tent of skin   each one
different yet similar   all maddeningly known
to me   And each neck grows into thrusting
in my direction   where I finally notice
that they are adorned with pendants   amulets
twisted into repulsive shapes   made of horn
    of beak and claw   And all together hang
like the snattering paws of virulent dybbuks
    hovering demons cryptically severed
from their own limbs
The muscles in my own arm twitch
yet they and their hands are powerless
to reach past the vile jewelry
to the proffered necks
I let go the last sack   A wind is up
in the yard   the sun wavers   a dancing whirlwind
of sawdust and leaves and feathers   all red
of a sudden   all wet   obscures everything
    clouds my willing eyes
Then I am awake
with the sun in my eyes
It is time for Morning Prayers

Some of these poems have been published, in one form or another,
in *Atlantic Advocate, Beloit Poetry Journal, Fiddlehead, First
Encounter, Poet, Porcépic, Salt, Waves* and in *Voices Down East.*
Some have been published in *Birthday,* a New Brunswick Chap-
book. A number have been broadcast on CBC radio.

Library of Congress Catalogue Card No. 74-76143

ISBN 0 88750 109 5 (hardcover)
ISBN 0 88750 110 9 (softcover)

Cover by Margaret Capper
Book design by Michael Macklem.

Printed in Canada at The Coach House Press

PUBLISHED IN CANADA BY OBERON PRESS

T6